In the short grass

In the short grass

HASKELL ROBINSON

authorHOUSE®

AuthorHouse™
1663 Liberty Drive
Bloomington, IN 47403
www.authorhouse.com
Phone: 1-800-839-8640

Published by AuthorHouse   03/11/2013

ISBN: 978-1-4817-2114-1 (sc)
ISBN: 978-1-4817-2113-4 (e)

Library of Congress Control Number: 2013903657

Any people depicted in stock imagery provided by Thinkstock are models, and such images are being used for illustrative purposes only.
Certain stock imagery © Thinkstock.

This book is printed on acid-free paper.

Because of the dynamic nature of the Internet, any web addresses or links contained in this book may have changed since publication and may no longer be valid. The views expressed in this work are solely those of the author and do not necessarily reflect the views of the publisher, and the publisher hereby disclaims any responsibility for them.

CHAPTER 1
IN THE SHORT GRASS

The season was changing, summer was going south and blustering autumn winds were charging into Boston, my hometown. A near decade of unrest in the neighborhoods was winding down. The "social experiment" implemented by outside carpetbaggers and liberals had failed miserably, leaving deep wounds to its people and their reputation. Forced integration of public school children without much planning, and inside knowledge of inner-city values caused a volcanic eruption of emotions that left a disaster in its wake.

South Boston to my east was almost maligned beyond repair for decades, and deemed a racial caldron of thugs. Education suffered greatly as rebellion took to the forefront. School children were forced to leave to leave the sanctity of a safe familiar environment, and dropped in places where cab drivers were afraid to pick up fares. The real fight was not over race, but mandated relocation to places the media had labeled dangerous and uninviting. Judge Garrity, of an affluent suburb to the west, had instigated the insanity to improve the quality of education in the city. The city wide experiment was a total failure and education suffered.

With the temperatures dropping, the timing could not have been better if the state had suspended us from our jobs a couple months earlier. A co-worker and I were given full paid leave. David pulled up to our triple decker about 9 a.m. each morning, leaned on the horn that briefly drowned out the sound of the base-thumping blast from his nearly 10-year-old 73 Chevy Caprice.

I scampered down three flights of narrow, winding stairs of the century old wooden structure that lined the street. I left as fast as possible with clubs and golf shoes in-tow so neighbors would not "make" the driver or car. Our tight knit neighborhood was forever vigilant about outsiders who entered. David, a black man, would not have been met with open arms. The car was huge, resembling a parade float with fat, white walls, sparkling paint and spoked-wheels immaculately detailed by hours of buffing and prepping. The inside was also tidy and smelled of the always-present cardboard-vanilla trees hanging all over the interior. He was obsessed with cars and enjoyed driving all over the state for our golfing matches on paid holiday. Over the years working with him, I had come to realize he was as crooked as a snake-in-a-hurry, and could never fully trust him to be honest.

I never introduced my golf partner to my mother, who occupied the second floor. She was very nervous around black men because of a few purse-snatch incidents while walking home, up the hill, usually on payday. We had both caught the "golfing bug", and were completely addicted, in a big way, to the game of skill and chance. Our first stop was always back to his neighborhood corner variety store for a nickel bag of pot, his jump start for the day. Drugs were dispensed from variety stores like candy and cigarettes "in the hood".

Golf had become our salvation in these "trying times" on full paid leave. Our battles took place out in the country far from the inner city, on beautifully manicured fairways cutting through forests. These well-kept green pastures of lush grasses captivated our long days for the outdoor pool game. I was a more skilled golfer because of early exposure as a golf caddy at a club in nearby Brookline, Mass., in the early seventies.

What David lacked in golfing talent he compensated with gamesmanship and "head trips". Exorbitant wagers could turn a man into an instant jellyfish, especially on our meager state salaries. It was not uncommon for our bets to reach one hundred dollars a hole, a sum that would make your knees knock over a four-foot putt to win. The external pressure of gambling on skill made you mentally stronger in competition. There was no such thing as "country club gimmies", everything had to hit the bottom of the cup. Collecting winnings from my opponent was always the most pressure, but a transaction did occur despite some convincing arguments. I played best at a fast, not-so-much to think about pace. David would deliberately slow things down to alter my tempo when taking command or about to go three holes up. He would press more than a Chinese laundry when I started to pull away. A press starts a brand new match from that point on, and also begins a new wager. A press can only be initiated when the golfer is down two holes in match play. David was a master of psychological warfare, often times having me so rattled the match was over before plugging the tee into the ground on number one. You had to take a guy like him in small doses or you'd be mentally disintegrated. He had manic energy when it came to verbal butchering. Our home track was the oldest public golf course in the country. Franklin Park was an all black course at the time, and my game and my money was always welcomed there. I learned everything about the game from highly skilled "ghetto" pros. I have yet to witness more exuberance and integrity towards the game of golf anywhere else in the world.

Although we only lived two miles apart as the crow flies, our city neighborhoods were extremely different and were segregated along the color lines. My neighborhood was situated on an enormous hill, with century-old wooden triple-deckers that were weathered and worn by severe New England seasons. They resembled weary old men standing shoulder to shoulder, leaning on each other before they would fall flat on their faces, forward. Some of these aging Victorians were neatly painted or slapped with aluminum siding to mend their rotted appearances. There were a few brownstone row houses sprinkled in against the decaying architecture.

Generations before, the flats of these great triple-deckers housed large immigrant families with many children. The Irish were the most prevalent, along with German, Greek and Albanians smatterings in the one square mile of Boston, named Mission Hill. Neighborhood unity and strong political clout achieved by numbers of registrants pushed out cops, fireman, city and state workers, court and correctional staff, longshoreman, iron workers and other union men. We had our very own state representative, home grown from these humble beginnings, to be a voice for the working families that may have needed a leg up when times were tough. I always wondered how nine children fit into three small bedrooms. My friends growing up would have to piss out a window or into a cup. Meals were conducted in assembly line fashion. The union and government jobs were passed to the children as a reward for staying true to the neighborhood, and not fleeing to the suburbs during the turbulent-forced busing crisis of the 70's. A politically appointed job usually spelled union wages, pension, annuity, and no heavy lifting.

In the early eighties, the neighborhood began a re-gentrification process. Outside speculators rolled the dice and began buying up the run down three deckers, transforming the rubble into real estate empires. Three houses in one and the proximity to downtown, several major colleges and four major Boston hospitals may have been all the insight they needed. They began to "doll up" the old tenements with fresh paint and renovations, turning the triple income flats into piggy banks. A few locals, mostly Greeks and Albanians also rode the wave of investment and rehab.

As the rents swelled thrice, the new faces began to appear. On paper, the speculators became millionaires, even surviving the crash of the late eighties; letting the bank take back a few of the unoccupied properties. Stavros across the street from me was a bellman at a downtown hotel and owner of millions of dollars in neighborhood properties. He was an old time mover and shaker; no time for childhood or adolescence; these formative years were spent in the streets making cash; shinning shoes and selling flowers by the hospitals; those were his gigs.

There were only a handful of neighborhood guys with this insight, and money to invest locally; the rest was outside money. The extreme rent hikes changed the neighborhood forever. Life long residents were forced out, as professionals and herds of students crammed into the working class neighborhood. Homeowners, who cashed in on the overnight real estate boom traded dilapidated triples for single family housing in the suburbs to the south. The newcomers to Mission Hill would fit better in Beacon Hill until reality set in.

The locals called the new breed of landlords and tenants "urban pioneers." These speculators came from all over the map to invest in and renovate the houses; most actually occupied a floor themselves if they did not have children to raise. The overnight rent increases paired with neighborhood displacement issues sparked an instant resentment. Those left behind could not afford to live in their own neighborhood. On the surface, the pioneers blended with the tough, working class Irish of two generations or more. They were white and they worked, much like an aspirin. The pioneering progress was responsible for breaking up a tightly-knit and insulated community.

Talk in the five neighborhood taverns was that we dropped the ball and fell asleep, letting the carpetbaggers ruin our neighborhood. I spent most of my twenties drinking and drugging in three local gin mills, a walking distance from my house. Not wanting to be alone when not working, the barrooms were family rooms for me to relax and stay up to date on the neighbors. My favorite stop was Ed Burkes on Huntington Avenue. This upholstered sewer-hole featured live bands and attracting plenty of women from outside neighborhoods and nearby suburbs. There was also local talent from the Baptist Nursing School program atop "The Hill". These young lovely's enjoyed our company and endless supply of cocaine. I recall the long hours of conversation about nothing of substance in between lines of bar room coke. A new variety of nurses were led to the slaughter every year or two, and in short time they were done with us.

The neighborhood was our priority, not much for holding hands for longer lengths of time. Most of the other four taverns were rough-and-tumble saloons, seldom visited by female patrons; a fine place for a beer and a bloody nose. Cocaine in the eighties ran like beer from the taps. Alcoholism and drug abuse was very prevalent to those of us remaining on ""The Hill". A city block from party central boasted Boston's highest crime rate of record. The crime zone was directly attributed to the two large housing projects that boarded the neighborhood since the early sixties. The concept of grouping poor and desperate people inside a brick maze was not a positive thing. The "bricks" surrounding Mission Hill led the league in homicides, drug activity and drug related crimes that generated money to pay for drugs. This proximity to a war zone was overlooked and not taken into consideration by the new investors on ""The Hill", causing at times a real culture shock. Often on a hot summer's night one could hear the pop, pop, of gun shots from the back of the Hill at Bromely Heath projects. There was so much press coverage on the Mission Hill project crime that many people did not realize there was also a neighborhood close by. Pools of ground up glass on the sidewalks from constant auto smash-and-grabs littered the landscape. Many a resident would awaken to their cars mounted on four cinder blocks minus tires, radio and anything else of value. There was always the occasional purse-snatching incident. House break-ins were an epidemic, and many of the new comers were targeted, as they were perceived as weaker people, not being "schooled" by the unpredictable and violent streets. The crimes were not only perpetrated by project thugs, but the few local men caught in the heroin trap, which was an everyday job to stay high once addicted. The coke, you could sleep off and go to work for more money only to feel lousy again in a few days. The neighborhood's safety on the physical hill itself had been improved by episodes of quick response teams, of as many as twenty young men, assembled and armed with bats, sticks, clubs and pipes to thwart attempted victimization of neighbors. The burglars, thieves, and purse snatchers now fell victim to swift street justice, leaving them bloodied and beaten before police and ambulance arrived to rescue them.

There was a strict "code of silence" when we were questioned by law enforcement, and most of the cops quietly agreed with our actions. The battle lines were drawn, and the predators searched for easier targets elsewhere. The students sent to Boston's Mission Hill for higher education were a source of instant entertainment as their new wave costumes were very amusing. Spiked pink hair with purple velvet dinner jackets, and Air Jesus sandals was their fashion statement. To go to school in Boston you had to come from money, and these students seemed to be rebelling against something. The city kids had to wear Adidas or Nike and shop high-end brand name clothiers.

David's neighborhood, two miles across town, saw no gentrification. The same 100-year-old Victorians crafted when labor was cheap, and skilled craftsman took painstaking time for innate mahogany carvings of mantles and trim, stain glass windows, remained in crumbling decay. This Dorchester neighborhood had many houses boarded up, red-lined and mired in complete urban desolation. The abandoned buildings provided shelter for homeless crack heads, junkies, and street hustlers. The more fortunate, respectful citizens enjoyed great opportunities to get ahead in the work force as affirmative action gave the minority community many advantages. These residents became policemen, fireman, union workers, and city and state employees. The housing values never escalated and kept many good people trapped in urban blight. The people of Codman Square couldn't make the big real estate cash-out that Mission Hill enjoyed, as this area was not yet desirable. It would be well into the next century until a substantial gentrification process occurred here.

These mean Dorchester streets were burdened with excessive gunplay and gang activity. Life had become very cheap. Teen pregnancy was extremely high and "babies having babies" was the catch phrase of the day. The crack cocaine epidemic plagued this neighborhood in the late 70's, and still today, lingers around the sick and suffering citywide Boston residents.

When David and I rode together in the buffed Chevy, we were met with mean stare downs from the Dorchester locals. This "cracker" had to be a cop, the enemy to most and a symbol of repression. Detectives with random pat frisks kept the courts and jails very busy. Although random searches were somewhat illegal, the police mentality was "pay a lawyer and tell the judge in Dorchester district". The neighbors viewed us as the five-o or fifty when we entered the hood. The salt and pepper team to shake down the residents. It was still very uncommon for different races to be together in the early 80's, in this Dorchester section. The crack cocaine menace grabbed David hard enough to bring a world-class athlete down to his knees. At the height of 6'10, he had incredible athletic prowess, a leading scorer for the Florida State Seminoles in his last two seasons. After a brief stint in A.B.A playing for the Las Vegas Gamblers, he headed off to Europe for 4 years, playing for all the major cities in the European League. He returned to Boston broke and still smoking crack. He had lost all body fat and resembled a telephone pole, still a good-looking one at that.

In 1979, David headed for Washington Street in Boston's Red light district, or combat zone, to peddle his merchandise. Pimping came natural to this mind control maniac. He always admired the older pimps as he grew up. Attractive young women who wanted to be emotionally and physically controlled were his prey. The Greyhound Bus terminal was a good place to pluck such an eager participant. Women looking for a strong father figure were a good catch. The women were treated like 7-year-old children, constantly monitored it in a cat and mouse type of game. Each woman wore an electronic beeper the size of a toaster oven and was constantly kept in check. They had to drop-a-dime in the phone booth after every trick or face severe discipline. They were not allowed to spend any of their hard-earned money, as goodies and things were bought for them by pimps. A safe place to live and the occasional new dress were the only rewards the women received. If they "produced" and were compliant they were led to believe David "loved" them and he treated them like a girlfriend.

In the 70's, there was much money to be made in Boston's combat zone; hookers and pimps were highly visible to the bustling night trade. The district was also home to Boston's

Chinatown. It would take a unified Chinatown, of merchants and neighbors, to almost 25-years to push the sex market merry-go-round out of their neighborhood. The adult "fun zone" landed on the avenues of Boston's still struggling neighborhoods and to the madams' of the Yellow page escort services.

One night, David was heading out of the combat zone in his older Mercedes, with his two workers on board, when he spotted the late great coach "Red" Aurabach at the light. He immediately began to sell himself to Red. He talked his way onto the parquet floor of the Boston Garden for a tryout. Red, in the early days, spent a lot of time scouting for the Celtics and had probably recognized him from his heroics in the annual Boston Shootout Tourney in the early 70's held at Northeastern University on Huntington Ave. He made the team despite his battle with the gorilla on his back, crack cocaine use. It was Larry Birds rookie season, a player we did not know much about. David had incredible ability for shooting and shot blocking. He told me on several occasions how he swatted Birds shots in the inner club scrimmages. He was cocky, bold and brash, toughened by street survival techniques, and the disease of addiction. I can picture him saying "in your face trash collector", amongst other obnoxious taunts. Bird probably was not used to "ghetto warfare" at that level.

That years Press book, for those who made the roster, was good to David even though he only lasted four games. The press book stated, "That if strictly shooting was the name of the game, he would have been awarded Birds contract money". He would glare hopelessly at the Press book quote in years to come, of endless crack-induced episodes. Wasted talent by a world-class athlete, with everything needed to succeed in the NBA except freedom from addiction. Alcohol, crack and cigarettes came between David and "the big time".

Today's golfing adventure brought us 20 miles south of the city. The long ride was spent talking about the kids in our charge, and of course, how much of an ass-whooping I was about to encounter on the links. We had worked at the state facility for violent juvenile delinquents. He was out on a disability after being kicked, breaking up a fight on the basketball court. I was suspended with full pay, accused of insubordination to a ranking officer. This officer, although, having no seniority or work-related experience, had won the supervisors spot to satisfy "the quota system" encouraged by affirmative action legislation. Someone always gets short-changed when there are quotas. Life is not always fair, especially in the work force. I resented her appointment and acted on it instead of accepting it as something I was powerless over. Several months with pay followed the incident.

The first day of my suspension on my shift, an extra ordinary riot, taking three police agencies to quell what erupted on my shift. The riot was covered by TV and newspaper media. I felt like my kids on the unit vindicated the unfair promotion and bullshit suspension.

The D.Y.S. facility was the States maximum-security rehabilitation center. Each unit would hold up 20 of the states most dangerously violent criminal teens. The crimes in my unit were murder, rape, armed robbery and assaults with dangerous weapons; nothing nice going on here. Around 1974 Dr. Jerome M. came to Boston and took control of the system. He deinstitutionalized children in lockup except for the extremely violent children who committed extreme atrocities. They no longer housed children who skipped school or were incorrigible at home, with the violent offenders. Three staff members without weapons or tactical police back-up force were to maintain order and assure the routines of prison life were followed. Handcuffs and leg irons were used for the aggressive and out of control inmates as well as for those who fought as they jockeyed for power and position. Our facility was like a mini penitentiary, without the yard and surrounding wall. There was a gym, weight room, and a pool with three feet of water inside. The old facility was the Lyman School for Boys that opened at the turn of the century, in rural Central Massachusetts. There were cottages with steel, wire grates on the windows to house the boys ranging from 7 to 18 years of age. Corporal punishment in the form of horrendous beatings was very common. Boys were made to stand at attention for days.

The job became more stressful and demanding when we had to break up fights, and restrain out of control children with handcuffs and leg irons. I did not enjoy this procedure, Our charges, for most, were never unified, and lucky for us, they were not. They could have easily overtaken three unarmed staff members. Your best defense weapon was the ability to think on your feet and stay alert for signs of trouble. The Department of Youth Services set out to hire big and intimidating-looking men to make things easier.

A man approaching 80-years of age told of the sexual abuse by staff and older boys to young lads. He had suffered many broken bones at the hands of sadistic guards, and was emotionally shaken at the recall of his treatment in the 1940's. He was a runner, a Charlestown street kid going on to rob banks and armored cars as many "Townies" before and after him. He told me of "clutching a machine gun and heading out to the school", but turning back, as he "did not want innocent blood on his hands".

David and I both were from the inner city. We both were large men, both having been in trouble with the law; another helpful prerequisite for employment. I earned the respect of the lads by giving respect and "Treat others how you want to be treated" was my motto. I dealt the kids as if I were in their shoes. When I had to use force and say, "pull the trigger," I did, and did not hold back to quell a disturbance to prevent a major incident. On our 3-11 shifts, there were less structured events for the boys as opposed to the day shift, which was spent in classrooms doing schoolwork. We had few major problems on our shift, although, we were not as strict as the first shift crew was. The crews on the day shift were like cowboys at a rodeo; military men or with a similar mentality would torment the kids so they could shackle and hog-tie them for sport.

I did not enforce all of the rules all the time. Discipline was a carefully planned balance; if too lenient, they would walk over you like a doormat, if too strict caused an angry rebellion. I managed to show the residents I cared about how they were treated, not becoming aggressive or violent; a sign of staff burn out. The more positive relationships formed on the unit, the easier the job was. David's presence on the unit was helpful as a former pro athlete, but he was not very proactive. He chose his 8-hour shift to catch up on some sleep or eat; things the progressive disease of addiction demanded from him. He would be up for days smoking crack and drinking, when his money permitted. The residents that were committed to our facility had the "Reject" stamp plastered in their foreheads. They needed to be kept away from society, in a place where they could be safely "sustained" like animals in a Zoo. These unfortunate kids were societies throwaways, a percentage that would that would always be in the system.

Most would spend the majority of life behind prison walls or die on tough city streets. Every few years one of the resident criminal escapades would be headline news in Boston. The most notorious inmate, even at present, in the state prison system, came through D.Y.S. Roslindale for most of his childhood years. We had watched an 11-year-old, committed youth's transformation into a predatory animal, still fighting the system vigorously 25-years later. He had made the local news for stabbing his lawyer and a nurse before a trial, in Dedham Superior Court, for the rapes of other inmates. He had his own move-team assigned to him, at "the prison within a prison", at the maximum security Walpole State.

It was early December, and despite the ground being nearly frozen we were still on our daily golf pilgrimage. You can get a lot of roll on the frozen turf this time of year. David had settled his worker's compensation suit, and I was forced to resign after 4 years of state service. The D.Y.S. Detainees were still our entertainment sources. If they only knew how much time we all spent talking about their crazy antics, mannerisms, and bizarre behaviors they would think they were celebrities.

The day after watching Escape From Alcatraz featuring Clint Eastwood, three white inmates, the entire white population, were noticed standing on the flat roof of the super max unit, while I parked my rust bucket in the lot. At first, it did not register what exactly was happening and I nearly dismissed it as disbelief. The inmates, like Clint, went up a ventilation shaft and got onto the roof. I entered the unit after passing through four, six-inch doors to hear a frantic day supervisor scream "I literally can't account for three inmates." I nonchalantly commented, "That may have been the residents spotted on the rooftop." The chase was on. Two residents were immediately captured and the third had jumped, holding a wire that snapped from high a top the roof, and was found unconscious the next day in the bushes below. I was assigned as an advocate for one of the captured kids. I thanked him for not pulling his shit on my shift. I treated this kid as if he were my own. Rehabilitation was unfortunately out of reach at this point in their lengthy criminal career.

I remember 15-years after my tenure at D.Y.S. Roslindale, of a very remarkable incident at Park Square. While waiting for the Red line subway train, eight young black men made a circle around me. I did not really recognize any of them and prepared for the worst. Instead of throwing me on the third rail to barbecue, one of the men reached out his hand for some skin and said, "Mr. Russo you were good to us and have a nice day". I thanked God immediately for my good fortune, trying not to show how truly terrified I was after "dodging a bullet", so to say.

CHAPTER 2
THE SUDDEN IMPACT

I n May of 1985, our beloved three family house traded hands to another get-rich-quick speculator from nearby Brookline. My "party palace" on the third floor was gone as the rents tripled. I was forced off to Brighton, getting a single room on the third floor of a triple-decker with two other roommates occupying the two additional bedrooms. I took a job driving a cab until I could catch a break with something more substantial.

The rental market high-atop Mission Hill began to escalate at the end of the decade, and the huge new rents were hard to fetch. A neighborhood drug dealer approached the out of town landlord, posing as a member of Local 33 Roofers Union and secured the downstairs unit with cash. This unit was the Cadillac of the house; all new fixtures and renovations. My mother would have spit blood if she knew that the new inhabitants were selling drugs from the house. She was like the many before, cashing out and running to the "burbs", far from the madness of the inner-city life.

Drug houses were very scarce in the mostly white, working class neighborhood. The neighborhood barrooms were where street drugs were usually dispensed. One or two dealers got "the nod" from tavern owners to provide the coke to stimulate drinking patrons trying to get back to even. The coke brought you up and the drink brought you down. A vicious cycle, but a boom for bar owners. Street smart, sober neighborhood dealers were allowed the privilege of selling grams and half grams of coke to people they knew. The dealers would never sell to an outsider or someone they did not know where they attended grammar school.

A constant flow of foot traffic began to parade into our old Frawley Street dwellings. It was getting to be like 7-Eleven, open 24-hours a day, seven days a week. The new big absentee landlord got his rents and the neighborhood got a rat poison factory on the block. Soon there was to be trouble in paradise. A local man concerned for the health of his wife, who was becoming an everyday customer to the nose candy cottage, decided to make a stand and administer a stern warning. Coke in the white neighborhoods was still predominately sniffed and not freebased into crack. Joseph was street tough with chiseled facial features, reddened by hours atop skyscrapers connecting steel and afternoons in the barrooms, at the bottom of "The Hill". He was tall and lean with large heavy weather-beaten hands, and he knew how to use them. His reputation as one of the neighborhoods better fighters was earned by the many street-fighting victories of the late 60's and 70's growing up; when everyone fought to gain respect. Those who avoided fighting in the street allied with tougher kids for a price. Untreated alcoholism can keep life long neighbors at war.

Josephs timing could not have been worse as he arrived on the back porch of my old digs. He had walked up on a carefully planned ambush and robbery, of the drug dealer he had come to reprimand. The robbery was orchestrated by two, hooded black males who were fairly certain that this dealer did not pack a gun for protection. Joseph confronted the two thugs at the door and instinctively knew what was up. The three men stood on the porch with entirely different intentions. Joseph acted first and threw a straight right to the jaw of the taller bandit and barked for the other to "fucking screw". The tall robber fell face first on the stoop as a single gunshot rang out in the still summer night. Joseph fell back and collapsed, dying instantly from a single bullet wound to the heart. The shooter and accomplice were later apprehended at the projects. The outside speculators economic hunch and our willingness to cash out in some way caused this chaos to happen and drop a bomb on the neighborhood.

The shooter was convicted of second-degree murder and received life with parole after 15-years, and his accomplice got life as well. The neighborhood coke dealer got pinched a year later and received a 10-year mandatory sentence. The real tragedy was that Joseph's family lost a good father and supportive husband. The neighborhood became white hot. Drug unit cops became highly visible after the shooting. The only neighborhood dealers to survive now would have to up the "pay off" to the local police to stay in business. It was not uncommon for a few tainted police to become cokeheads or overly greedy for money.

The room I took in Brighton was clean, safe and affordable. The neighborhood was transient and full of B.U. and B.C. students. There was an "Easter basket" of ethnicities crammed together. I was able to drive a cab every other day and golf on the days off in-between. I enjoyed the freedom of driving a cab in Boston and picking my spots. I worked 4:00 pm to 4:00 am, staying very busy after midnight; mostly because my competition had put up for the evening. After midnight, the underground economy of drug transactions and female escorts seemed to keep me busy. Many third shift workers also used cabs to get to their jobs in hospitals and factories. The late shift was steady money with little traffic to contend with. The weekend bar closing was very profitable, along with trips to the many drug houses in the city. I knew where every drug house was located before long. I had lost contact with David and his domineering style of friendship. There are two kinds of people, "givers and takers "and we were at different poles here."

I had a chance run-in with David two years down the line in 1987. He was driving a cab and parked in Boston's busy Kenmore Square. The Square catered to college students and younger crowds that filled the many nightclubs and bars. We both were surprised to see that each of us had regressed to driving a cab, and stopped in a cafeteria for a bite to eat. As usual, everyone stopped what they were doing to gaze at the slender 6'10 black man, who could have been a fashion show model. We discussed the idea of starting a Limousine Service in the city of Boston. I was all ears and eager to start out on my own at the ripe age of 27. David had great salesmen-ship demeanor and qualities. He always introduced himself as the former Boston Celtic and International Basketball star. He was an eloquent speaker and good at convincing others. "The first three letters of the word convince should be aptly noted." He no doubt had that special aura about him. He was conditioned in the streets of the ghetto, but also educated by his worldly European basketball experiences.

David had the line of credit and I had some cash stashed to get three limousines up-and-running. He had a long-time family friend let us use a garage in one of the Boston's worst, and most dangerous urban areas. Every other house was boarded up. It looked like Beirut after and overhead bombing mission. Each morning, male and female crack heads would line up at the garage and try to sell their merchandise or "services" to the working men at the garage. You can be creative with the later. Inside the garage, it was like fucking Sears Roebucks, as the merchandise piled up. We paid pennies on the dollar, acquiring hot items for a fraction of its worth. Put David in an Armani Suit wlth his good looks, trim athletic build, and a few A-A slogans about recovery and we started to acquire major corporate accounts. People liked to hear a man on "the comeback trail", even if he was professing a crock of shit. Our competition was the

19

Boston taxi industry and their pathetic drivers. The traveling corporate men were not happy with the poor service of the cab industry and the black car service was moving strong into the suburban airport transportation field.

The black car service to Logan Airport was becoming increasingly popular. The executive transportation business was ours to make or break. I had stopped all my drinking and drugging to focus on the prospect of legitimate business. Making money was how my new compulsion of the day. Corporate and residential airport transportation got the company up and rolling and off the ground. Our inside joke campaign slogan was "Don't get taken by a Jamaican". We added more vehicles and vans to accommodate the growth spurts. We also aligned with other small companies to help sub-contract each other's overflow, when we all over booked.

To celebrate "our" new successes, David bought a one-bedroom condominium 25 miles west of Boston, in the old boot-making town of Marlborough. The unit was small. Even though David had 11 children by four different women, his kids were not a huge priority at this time in his life. A feisty woman name Charlene, who had 3 of his children, pursued him as best she could for support. She wound up helping us in the office with bookings and reservations. She was a silent sufferer, managing three children under 10-years-old, without financial help aside from meager state programs, and a small, sporadic salary from our limousine company. I realized how strong and resilient some black women had to be to survive. David was a "rolling stone" and the women he bedded down accepted that and settled for less.

CHAPTER 3
UPWARD MOBILITY

David enthralled the local town media with his former Celtic stint, and by now, stellar business accomplishments. He really knew how to make a big splash in the small, puddle of a city Marlborough Ma. The townspeople were certainly not ready for our big-city razz-mataz, but seemed very welcoming and hospitable on the surface. I felt like more of a silent partner, being greatly overshadowed by the "star of our show". It did not bother me, as down the road, being in the limelight would have adversely affected me. I knew with David's active addiction that I had to take charge of daily operations, and step up control of the Boston business in the Dorchester garage. You can take the man out of the city, but you can't take the city out of the man. David's old M.O. surfaced behind the smoke screen of his new suburban residence. We plugged in with a high-priced escort service that needed girls transported for their suburban calls.

The service was based in Newton MA., a very respectable and affluent town on the Boston line to the west. The "art" of pimping had not gone away and he soon commandeered two, one thousand dollars a day workers for his own stable. This shortcut to easy money triggered a full-blown addictive breakout. The ship was listing heavily. Smoking coke, excessive drinking, and out of control gambling were now everyday, all day obsessions. He was in the midst of a full-blown relapse. He would only break to keep the stable happy; being hung like a farm animal was a plus.

I soon discovered that most of the working gals did not really enjoy sex with men at this point in their tragic lives. They seemed to enjoy the kinder, gentler experience of another woman when they wanted true love. One gal explained to me "that's why we call the John's tricks, because that is what we are really doing to them". I kept the business running as best I could to make sure the crew met all the bookings, keeping the cars clean and maintained at all times.

All the money went through David's hands, and it was like lighting a match to it His booze, drugs and gambling became a 1500 dollar a day habit. Because there was so much cash in our daily operations, I always siphoned a weeks pay for myself. The repo men circled the fleet like vultures waiting for an opportunity to pounce. On a cold December day, I came out of the grocery store to find all four tires slashed on the biggest stretch limo in our shrinking fleet. Score one for the repo men as their flatbed tow truck got there in minutes. They did not have the berries to come to our garage in the ghetto.

The addiction strained our personal and business relationship greatly. I had reached the boiling point and my long rope had snapped. I confronted him at the Dorchester garage with a verbal barrage. After spitting on him, a fistfight broke out that eventually turned in W.W.F. wrestling match that spilled down the stairs in the front hallway. As I lay winded atop David I heard the click, click of a gun being cocked and felt the cold steel barrel of a shotgun, on the back of my neck. I strained from my breath. Marcus, a large black man, who shared the garage for repairs bellowed out in a deep baritone growl, "drop the shot gun, this beef ain't about race". I peeled myself up slowly and turned to thank Marcus for intervening in my apparent, intended decapitation. He shook his head smirking and said "get the fuck out of here you got too much crazy heart". He knew all along I wasn't pumping cool aid in my veins.

David's big mistake was stealing the women from the Newton escort service. The owner or madam was married to a high ranking Newton police officer. Mindsey's All-American girls service, along with Newton and Marlborough Police were now seeking revenge on A-cut Above Limousine service for our prostitute pilfering. Two undercover Marlborough officers posing as out of town, businessmen initiated the sting operation. They hired a stretch limo for the evening and requested David to drive if possible, baiting with a little extra something for his appearance. The detectives were looking for some action and inquired about a price for two girls for the entire evening. David quoted them 1200 hundred and the two lovely's were brought to the hotel for service, which should have been a red flag.

Hotels and motels are set-ups as opposed to the privacy of a man's house. The residential rendezvous proved over the years to be a safe bet.

Despite the girls asking to see some kind of identification, and then abruptly leaving the scene when they failed to comply, David was solely indicted for pandering and white slavery charges. His previous convictions of the same charges in the 70's did not help the situation. Immediate action was taken to revoke our license to operate out of the city of Marlborough, by the board of selectman, in a kangaroo court hearing. The same media that blew wet, fat kisses to us, had a field day slinging dirt balls at our company. Because of the enormous press coverage, we were politely asked to vacate all of our major corporate accounts. This was the biggest news of the year for this small city. We had crossed the wrong madam.

David made a plea bargain to avoid legal costs in district court, and received a slap on the wrist. After the media blitz, the company was ruined and quickly history. One of the stretch limousines was mysteriously stolen before we went under, to help us on the way out. Massachusetts led the nation in auto theft and subsequent insurance fraud. We hid the limo until we got the insurance payment and then resold it to a chop shop. The other five vehicles were left for the repo men. David's Marlborough condo was now in foreclosure. He packed his bags and headed for Atlanta to try his luck down south. I was left with a late model Lincoln town car with a bank note, and no capitol or corporate accounts. David received seventeen thousand for the limo and eventually I grabbed forty-five hundred for the parts up in Chelsea. I started to drive for the escort services full time trying to survive the wreckage of the company failure. I went with a busy service eight miles north of Boston in Revere. I made a weeks pay driving for several woman to their appointments in the suburbs with doctors, lawyers, dentists, judges, and regular Joes; who could afford the 200 an hour hit.

Although billing for an hour, most of the experienced girls were out of the house and on to the next "romantic experience" in less than 10 minutes. If the girls encountered a problem with a trick, they were to put 911 in my pager, as cell phones were non-existent in 1989. This never played out in my two-years of driving, but if it did I would be sure to drive as far and as fast away as possible. There was no big red "S" on my chest; Superman was not available, not for 30 dollars a call. One of the most lucrative accounts was a very prominent insurance broker, out in the pristine New England town of Concord. Every Friday night he placed an order for two men and two women to role-play sick, family incestual situations. He also ordered 6 grams of cocaine, another way for me to pad the pill. He kept the workers busy for about ten hours. I would gather the sex slaves the next morning at his insurance firm. The principles looked worn out and disgusted when the mission was completed, still windsurfing from all the cocaine they sniffed.

On Monday, Jerry V looked like a normal businessman, as I collected the five thousand dollar service fee he had probably skimmed from his company. The count was always right, 5 G's on the nose. Ms. Tiffany was my favorite hooker, although, I never sampled the product, it was all business. Ms. Tiffany was a former Vegas showgirl in her late 40's with a nice, well rounded figure. Her face was starting to show her age but that never slowed her down. She was like a utility player when it came to business. She lied about her age, hair color and weight, measurements to fit every request. She got in and passed right into work on every call, as she was close enough for every John. She was out in 10 minutes maximum, and on to the next call, a real "old school hustler". She said she was putting her daughter through college. This was probably a lie to gain my respectability, as we became casual friends. I could care less as I didn't judge her for her work. I know one thing; she stood apart from most, as she did not have a drug or alcohol problem.

Her worst day, and most unsettling episode happened in Foxboro, 20 miles south of Boston, where she was entertaining two Johns; one of them slipped out one of the thin rubber condoms, separating Ms. Tiffany from her and her so detested tricks. She was in a panic state, sprinting out of the house half naked and cursing the high heavens. She was in a complete fit of rage about what had happened. A man's semen entering her was taboo and could be dangerous with the diseases it carried. She was done for the day and in an emotional wreck for the long ride back to Revere.

I had disengaged any true feelings for my clients, as deep down I did not approve of the way they were degraded and used for money. In two year's time, saving enough money to get two additional cars and start Brighton Limo and car service, living as a minimalist, and not indulging in the party life were the keys to my savings. I learned a great deal about business and how to market from our failed limousine company; "you learn more from your mistakes." In the late 80's, Boston's Logan Airport was still new to the concept of organized limo pick-up of passengers. Things were not regulated strictly at this point, and MassPort police were easy targets. For a small bribe they would go down the cab line and produce a transfer, over 100 dollars for my black sedan. I never left the airport empty and often dead-headed to the airport to solicit the myriad of lost or stranded passengers, for a fair price. I never really price-gouged or stole from other services that had legitimate reservations. I provided service for the lost, forgotten and impatient traveler trying to get from point A to point B. Convincing people to use the "gypsy" limo was an art that I perfected over time. I was not alone, but compared to N.Y.C. there was only a fraction of independent operators playing the airport as N.Y.C. was years ahead of Boston, as the "black gypsy" Limos were often hailed on the streets.

The Japanese tourists were loaded down with money at that time and became marks for all the airport hustlers. This was too good of a score to resist. One day, two Japanese businessman wanted to go shopping at the outlets. We wound up in Kittery, Maine for a day. They were happy to pay me nine hundred dollars for the day's excursion to the North. I rationalized the price as payment for my exceptional hospitality and historic New England narration. The two black cars stayed primarily focused on sucking Logan's fruitful trees of disorganized ground transportation.

Both I and driver Billy dressed the part. We wore suits and had neat crew cuts, touting two way radios to look as official and as in place as possible. We spent long hours asking hundreds of people a day where they were going and what service they were looking for. We miraculously happened to have a cancellation and an open car to get them there, for the price quoted in the Hackney book that we both carried. People at Logan were vulnerable; they wanted to get home and fast. The late model Sedans, radio contact, and our professional appearance made our four hundred dollar a day hustle a reality. This was also a great place to network and get exposure. More established Limo companies would give us their overflow to handle. Brighton Limousine made money claiming back former corporate accounts and adding some large, new ones.

The new company targeted the very rich-and-famous men in the Commonwealth. We kept the two black Sedans running around the clock and brokered the overflow work, minus 20% for the house. In the beginning, we still provided service for the working girls. It was not uncommon to drop the Cardinal off at the Brighton Archdiocese and grab a prostitute for a rendezvous in Milton with a judge. We did not discriminate, going from hookers to holy men in the same hour. Forming lasting relationships with corporate leaders was key to our success. My theory "keep the men at the top happy and the rest of the account would follow like sheep". Never send a subcontractor to pick-up a CEO or a major player. The corporate giants loved being coddled, and we tried to pamper them the best we could. Doughnuts, coffee, their daily newspaper, radio station and interior temperature were suddenly important when they were onboard. We were always sub-servant to the customers. We never spoke unless spoken-to. It was their ride and they paid top-dollar for the experience. If the client did not want to engage in meaningless small talk, it was their choice.

The head of the Archdiocese of Boston was a very business-like man, resembling more of a CEO than a spiritual leader. He was very interested in the clank of the collection plates in all the cities and towns in predominately-Catholic Massachusetts. His Eminence and his trusted aid, the

Monsignor, discussed strategies of how to extract more revenue from the struggling parishes of the state. The back seat of my Lincoln was now a boardroom for some heavy-hitters in the business community. Organized religion certainly qualifies as big business. The Cardinal and his top aides treated me very well, always generous tips and hand rolled Cuban cigars. I was always invited in to dine with them, when we surveyed New England or drove to New York City. The money would be recycled in the near future, as my girls would be attending Catholic schools to avoid the sub-standard inner-city public schools. The church was suffering a tremendous scandal at the time. Some priests were indicted for child sex abuse and the Cardinal allegedly had the information, but did not act to have them removed; they went on to victimize other young boys. It was not my place to judge. I just kept my mouth shut and did my job. The scandal destroyed Cardinal Laws reputation in Boston and he could not be touted as a reference for me. I truly believe the decision not to act came from Rome; Cardinal Law was just a middleman, forced to obey.

Another huge corporate account at that time was New Balance Athletics Shoe Company. Jim D. and his wife were sole owners of this athletic shoe giant. Imagine that, mom and pop ownership at the billionaire level. There are no stockholders. It is a sole proprietorship. Public share holders not involved with corporate decisions. Jim bought the Watertown shoemaker in 1973 for a mere hundred thousand dollars. He was a shrewd, hardworking, second generation Greek, raised in Brookline. He had real "class" and carried himself like the star that he was. When he walked, he sauntered, like a thoroughbred race horse to the winners circle to accept the victory wreath. He kept himself in tremendous physical shape with workouts and proper diet. He had the aura of greatness, but he did not forget his roots.

I would often wonder, how this fucking guy pulled the whole thing off, to amass an empire like New Balance? Did he ever sleep? Did the saints bless him? Did he pray? How in the name of God do you organize a billion dollar giant? He must have had steel balls. He never used the big pro-athlete money-sucks for advertising like his competitions. What started as a working mans sneaker now was evolving into the trendy hundred dollar-a-pair athletic shoe of his competition. It was rumored that he took a 100 million dollar a year salary and why not? He was, however, not pretentious; still shopped at Marshalls for clothes. He probably shined his own shoes and cut coupons from the Sunday Globe.

Reebok was another corporate account of mine that kept Brighton Limo moving. Reebok had all kinds of money set aside for endorsements and we often carried pro-basketball stars to the airport from the Canton headquarters. The corporate travelers were not cash-money people, so we billed the tips directly to the company. The log book was always with reservation for ground transport and I was becoming a legitimate success story.

The Ryder Cup improved things considerably when it rolled into Brookline in 99 for a week. Brighton Limousine netted 25 thousand for the week for the transport services; six cars were booked around the clock while financial moguls followed their golf heroes at Brookline Country Club, battling the Europeans. Our guests stayed in the many five star hotels in the area and dinned each evening in Boston's most exclusive restaurants. The tournament cleared nearby Allen Farm for the hospitality tent and ground transportation area. I never saw such a spread of food and amenities assembled under huge tents that seemingly ran for miles. The golf officials were snobby and aloof to our crew of uniformed drivers, parked outside the tents. We were forbidden to enter any white tented functions. I met an old high school buddy from Mission Hill, who was now a cop on detail for the gala event. He slipped me a pass that enabled me to roam freely into the hospitality tents and experience the most elaborate spread of food I had ever seen.

My first stop was a photo opportunity with one of my favorite golf celebrities, Chi Chi Rodriguez. If Lee Trevino were there I would have been happier than a fag in Boy's town. Chi Chi was a great showman and ambassador to golf. After small talk and pleasantries were exchanged with Chi Chi, I was off for a luncheon snack. I began by sawing through a large center cut of a juicy prime rib while sipping Dom Perrignon champagne. The hospitality "snob" police abruptly halted my fine dinning experience. A tightly wound Yankee elitist tapped me on the shoulder and asked me to vacate my plate and follow her out of the tent for a word. She did a robot-like pirouette and waddled her ankle skirted fat ass towards the open field. She began the interrogation by asking me sarcastically, "What corporation do you represent"? She was floored when I produced not only a pass, but a VIP ticket from my lapel. Her face contorted and spun to the left before the stammering apology was delivered. I dusted myself off and reentered the festivities, unrattled by the misunderstanding. I was driving for the owner of Basset Broyhill Furniture in North Carolina for the tournament. Duane was a real Okie from Muskogee; the cowboy hat, boots and a southern drawl that added 2 or 3 syllables to his every word. My intentions with him and his wife were to get them out walking or sightseeing when away from the Ryder Cup. In the car, the tourists could see everything of interest in Boston in about 1 hour. You had to be creative if you wanted the hourly rate to rack-up.

The North End, a "slice of Italy" and adjacent Faneuil Hall, an open market place, could easily keep them busy for hours with dinning, and walking the brick path Freedom Trail. This guy had a lot of class, tipping me a deuce (200) when I dropped him off at Logan for his journey back to the woods.

CHAPTER 4
GO EAST TO SOUTHIE

I got married in 1991 to an attractive, city schoolteacher I meet at a hotel dance out in Brookline. We settled in South Boston, on the ocean side of the town, renting the second floor of a triple decker row house near the beaches. Our goal was to save for 3 or 4 years and then buy a house around Southie or Dorchester. Juanita and I both worked very hard towards the American dream of home ownership.

Southie was just a place for me to sleep. I was oblivious to any neighborhood happenings. The local Tribune reported each week about the plague of high-grade, cheap heroin that flooded into the neighborhoods. Each week several South Boston teens were overdosing or committing suicide, mostly by hanging because of the dope problem. Keeping a low profile and focusing on business were my priorities. It could have been South America for all I knew; I was almost totally detached from any street problems. Whitey Bulger, the Southie legendary gangster, was on the way out and was only newsprint to me. He stuffed many envelopes for the local police. I felt very comfortable living in Southie, close to the Logan Airport where the new 18 billion dollar tunnel made it a 2-minute commute to Logan. The only visible discord in town was over parking spots.

Attached three-family row-houses had no driveways and street parking was a "who got there first" war. Unlike Mission Hill, everyone owned a car in Southie. In the winter, you shoveled a spot on the public street and lay claim to it with just about anything imaginable as a marker. There were many chairs, trashcans, tea sets, desks, lamps or orange cones lining the shoveled parking spots. Extreme violence and car vandalism were typical responses for not honoring an erected monument for parking in Southie. The big difference from Mission Hill and Southie is that there were very few minorities in this town.

The projects were starting to slowly become integrated with Blacks and Hispanics. I observed white on white crimes for the first time, at 33 years-old. You could not blame black drug addicts over here. Whites committed all the housebreaks and robberies. Truck hi-jacks and smash-and grabs on Newbury St., the Rodeo Drive of Boston, were committed by gangs of Southie guys. Whitey had piece of all the drugs that moved through town, along with other organized criminal enterprises like gambling, loan-sharking, and big robberies. He had fought his way to the top of the heap of Southie. As for the 11 books recently written, he remained untouchable, as an informant or rat to all the other major crime factions in Boston. He had made a "pact with the feds" for immunity to commit crimes as long he continued to rat out his crime competition. Fifty-two low-level drug dealers were swept-up in an early morning March raid, and all reported directly to Bulger. Local cops wallets were also stuffed and good cops were told hands off "uncle Charlie" as Christmas was for kids and cops.

My marriage had been rocky from the start. Boston was a very expensive city and most couples needed a dual income to survive and save. Golfing had become a distant memory, as there was no longer life in the short grass for me. My career lasted about 10 years, posting a money spot in the 1993 Boston open Professional Golfers Tourney, shooting 73. A check for thirteen dollars was framed, never cashed. I was 35th in a field of 74, mostly Nike tour pros.

Our first daughter Andrea was born during a blizzard, in March of '93'. My life was altered 180 degrees at age 32. The business was growing like a wild fire; and with tight quarters, things were getting dicey. Having no family in the immediate neighborhood, things were rough. This factor is key to the disintegration of the modern American Family. Cousins, Aunts, Uncles, and Grandparents are non-existent, spread all over the country.

My wife had a perfect solution; move in Auntie Garcia. She spoke no English at all. My wife was of Cuban descent, so Auntie Garcia only spoke Spanish. I knew one thing; that she immediately detested me and that should have been a coming attraction as to what my wife must have filled her head with; stories of the "anvil" around her neck she married. Taking reservations from the house for the busy Brighton Limousine upset the family balance. I needed family members to stop making noise so I could book things properly on the mobile phone. The money was abundant and easy to save; there was no time to spend it. I took the family out to see some of the mansions my clients lived in. When we got to Mr. New Balance's house, my wife asked "How many families lived in this housing"? She had never been, nor had reason to leave the inner city to see how the other half lived. We did manage many trips throughout the 12-year marriage; to the Caribbean aboard cruise ships when I had a good crew to run the business.

In 1994, we bought a very elegantly-restored single family house, in a good section of Dorchester, Savin Hill, over the bridge. A ship builder from the Victorian era, using wooden ship beams for structural support for the floors, originally built the house. The century-old property came with a driveway, one and half acre of land, which was unheard of for most inner city houses. Auntie Garcia did not make the journey to nearby Dorchester and found another house to haunt, with other relatives. Our second daughter Angela arrived soon after the move. Some kind, elderly women in the neighborhood helped with children's needs, and things got better with the larger living space.

Making legit money was not enough for my greedy little hands, and I participated in an embezzlement scam of an elderly Jewish man, whom was over 100-years-old. I attribute all my downward spirals to this particularly bad karma-causing scam. Mr. Joleson needed to be constantly attended to, by caretakers, like an infant. These caretakers not only changed his diaper but also were in control of his banking assets and checkbooks. This old Brookline tycoon was a land baron in Metro-Boston, amassing a small fortune. Mr. Joleson's penchant was going to strip clubs each day, for 3 or 4 hours. The caretakers would launder large checks every day through Brighton Limousine. He was spending forty thousand a month on Limo services, at the end, before passing away suddenly of natural causes. Can you imagine, how pathetic to have lap dances daily at 104-years-old? He was very happy when he went. We were all in tears; our score went out the window.

In 1996 the business expanded. I rented an office on busy Dorchester Ave., trying to relieve tension on the home front. The Ave as it was called was a three-mile commercial strip that cut the length of the largest Boston neighborhood. It started in historic Lower Mills, home to the Baker chocolate factory, America's first, which came to a screeching halt at Broadway in Southie. Every store imaginable lined both sides of this busy thoroughfare. In recent years, the Vietnamese had made it "their" Ave, to accommodate the Vietnamese population explosion. A popular Boston Politician, Dapper O'Neil, was reprimanded by media for commenting while marching in the Dot Day parade that "he thought he was in fucking Hanoi". The Red Light district also began to crawl up and down the busy Ave. Pimping had gone out with sword fighting. These "freelance women of the night" paid only their drug dealers. It was a match made in heaven; all up and down The Ave drug houses flourished.

Turn a trick . . . . purchase a hit. The lawmen of District C-11 in Dorchester had their hands full, as more street walkers flooded The Ave at all hours, every day, to feed their drug habits. The police would at times create stings to curb The Ave of "sex for sale". I remember the police decoy-hookers as being always very to-good-looking to be real hookers, but they usually ensnared the suburban "John's". Across the street from my office was a block of Antique Furniture and Junk shops, owned by a great, large, Dorchester family. My phone and reservation book were now a fixture at Stuck in Time Antique Shop, my newfound sanctuary.

The owner of the shop was a fringe wise-guy or what we called "wanna-be" gangster or fangster (fake gangster). Sean did, however, beat a 7-year daily bout with heroin addiction. He was active in the smash-and-grab epidemic on Newbury St., and heists in the sprawling container-truck yards of South Boston, when he was an active user. He had been clean for 5-years when I met him, and he was fully loaded; with a ton of baggage and resentments for the 7-years he spent in reverse. You can take the rum out of the fruitcake, but you still have the fruitcake. Sean was an angry, dry-drunk. He had not spent more than a few days in jail for the million he and his crews robbed from the trucks in Southie.

Almost all kinds of "goodies" could be found in the large container-trucks; from laptops to designer suits. It was rumored that Sean had flipped on his crew, as they all had received lengthy prison sentences for various robberies. He was a shrewd businessman, as most of the furniture and collectables were removed from old Victorian attics as a favor to the homeowner. He had a very well-educated eye for what was desirable, never showed emotion as he cherry-picked the stand-out pieces that were heaped in with the worthless junk. The old furniture and gadgets from days gone by fascinated me, upon their arrival. The worthless trinkets found venue three doors down, into his brother's junk shop. Steve's place dealt mainly in trash pickings from the streets. He managed to do very well with it. The profit margin was enormous and he would often run into things of real value that was discarded on the curb. The two brothers never put a price tag on anything, as value was "yet to be determined" by the customers' response when viewing the piece. As in most antiques sales, bartering was a key element. If the customer seemed excited with a piece they would "bark out" a high price and tell them "this ain't no yard sale, try to get this price on Newbury Street." Remember, these stores were on Dorchester Ave, a rough-n-tumble inner-city landscape, and some of the customers invoked instant comedy to the locals.

Arthur and Bruce would walk/stroll in hand in hand, asking about a certain armoire or mahogany headboard, with a swishy, South End lisp. We were all warned not to torment or torture these well groomed and dressed young men, because they spent lots of money on this overpriced crap. Gay men were safer on this block than anywhere else in the free world. Although, I had often stepped over passed out junkies to get into the front door, this hang out broke up the long days I spent coordinating and driving corporate clients around the state.

The drugs brought problems to The Ave, as money was in constant need. A thief came by Stevie's to sell some hot tools. Stevie noticed a certain tool had a friend of ours' name tapped on the power drill. He tried to wrestle the drill away from the junkie thief. Without hesitation, and more like a reflex, I landed a left hook to the jawbone. We heard a pop like a water balloon breaking and watched him fall face first on the sawdust-covered floor. His jaw was broken and he was out cold. We carried the lifeless body out to the sidewalk, called 911, and carefully stuck a box knife in his hand. We corroborated our stories of the vicious attack we had just survived. A police officer accompanied the suspect into the ambulance and quickly ran a radio check to discover many arrest warrants, making us feel a little better.

Each shop also had rental units atop the store fronts to subsidize their incomes. Most of the tenants were down trodden, heroin addicts, supported by the state. Each month like clockwork, another tenant would overdose and die on this block. The neighborhood right-wingers would remark that these rental units cleansed the neighborhood of the riff-raff. Despite the Dorchester comeback, through revitalization and in-flux of urban professionals, this section of The Ave was still a hot mess.

CHAPTER 5
INEVITABLE

Tensions on the home front became unbearable. My long working hours chasing a buck strained our relationship. My hot-blooded Spanish wife was always upset about something and we distanced from each other. My relationships with my two young girls, "the two angels", kept my spirits high and filled the gap of a lonely marriage. Juanita had wanted out of the marriage for a long time, unbeknownst to me. She had been seeing a high-powered lawyer who represented all the fallen teachers of the Boston Teachers Union, a very tenacious and formidable force in the state. She announced the divorce declaration, and wanted everything in the settlement. She knew in the state of "Missusgetstochooseit" that she would prevail by playing the game. They played hardball, using anything and everything to gain the assets we had accumulated in a 12-year ride to the upper-middle class status.

Day one, I settled immediately on an inherited dual cemetery plot, conceding both plots to her in front of the judge, as long as she used her plot immediately. The judge was not amused at my attempt at levity and scowled an angry look in my direction.

Her lawyer was a portly woman with wild, kinky, salt and pepper colored hair, escaping in all directions. She had an enormous round face, wearing large, round, thick glasses. Physically she was not blessed with anything appealing to the eye; her dress did not gain her any points aesthetically. She wore tattered old dungaree smocks that hung off her like tent awnings. Her legs were never shaved; and almost always planted in earth shoes from the 70's. Everything about her demeanor exuded pure hatred of men. My wife had picked the top-gun in an all out campaign of terror against manhood. She was in my face the moment I laid eyes on her; this overstuffed Mamma Cass on a bad hair day. "You get those three Lincoln Town cars out of her driveway today by 5 or I'll have them towed!", was her initial greetings. "If you want your office supplies they will be placed on the sidewalk on Sunday between 2-4pm.!" The moment I hired my lawyer, a restraining order and a prevention order was issued, sending me packing. All of the allegations and the affidavits were totally fabricated and co-signed by Ana Klein, her partner in my eminent doom. The affidavits reported acts of physical violence, emotional torture, stalking, drug addiction, drunkenness, and money control.

In the Boston Probate court, no physical evidence or investigation was necessary and pure hearsay evidence was all that was needed. There was not a judge in Massachusetts that would risk their career by not issuing the stay-away order. The probate court was also a political "Hack-arama" dumping ground. I was sent fleeing with just the clothes on my back, instant homelessness. In shock, the thought of leaving my two adorable, young girls hit me like a ton of bricks; the feeling of being used and betrayed, the suddenness of all the events taking place. I never saw it coming. I was living in denial far too long. Almost to the end, she had plans of us investing in other multiple family houses together.

I somehow stayed glued enough to keep the business up and running, despite living in cheap motels on the city outskirts for the first few months. As long as she got to keep the house, I was allowed to see the girls every other weekend. In two months time, I was meeting the children 100 yards down the street out in the front of my newly purchased apartment complex.

If Tommy Hilfiger could buy the house across the street from his ex down in CT., I could buy a condominium down the street from my mine, in Savin Hill. I had promised the kids I was going to stay in the neighborhood and next door was available. My wife and her hired hit-dog protested about my new residence, but on the surface they couldn't really stop the move. The children were very happy to have their loving father in the neighborhood, so they could spend time with both their neighborhood friends and me.

They steam rolled over me like Germany invading Poland. My wife and attorney used the children and law enforcement to regain control of the battle and beat me into further submission. The duo scheduled a court appearance asking that she have total custody on the grounds of an unfit parent. I raced to the courthouse that day, but it was the wrong courthouse and the slaughter went on without me. The judge was not pleased with my mistakes I had made 25-years earlier, when my addiction was active. My past finally reared its ugly head and I was demonized for the duration of the "Kangaroo Court".

At times I had acted like an animal in the streets, but was always a gentleman in the home. Road rage could be attributed for a lot of my shenanigans. It had yet to be diagnosed. The court ruled 100% in favor of my wife, and the ever present "Godzilla" whose appearance fees were picked up by the City of Boston Teachers Union. This was another factor in the seemingly impossible struggle for fair play, as my tab went quickly to 15 grand. The children were devastated, trying their best to protest. They took the non-visitation as a death in the family; we were all in a mourning phase. My "charming" wife was being well coached by her lawyer and the children were being systematically brainwashed by an experienced schoolteacher.

Andrea, only 10-years-old was not fooled, speaking her mind by telling Juanita to "stick it where the sun don't shine". Angela bought the brainwashing on the surface for security reasons. It was better to take the side of the nurturing mother, for now. My lawyer was not effective in the Boston Probate arena. I became very lonely and depressed. I began to tune out the world using prescription painkillers to help me through the storm. I was now physically addicted to the pills, not realizing that stopping cold turkey induced a crippling depression. The new condominium purchase was a grave mistake because of the proximity to Juanita, and it was unfit for multiple inhabitants.

The walls of my new condo were paper-thin. The residents seemed like misfits and assorted mental patients. The lady to my left would call the police if I was snoring too loud. I could hear the people upstairs, every move and conversation. The police have to investigate noise in Boston and they were at my condo two times a week. I was becoming a pain in the ass for Dorchester Police. I knew the restraining order had also drawn the heat as the boys in blue never got to know me before my exit from the 13-year marriage;

Dorchester Police see life and people at their worst moments and they became very cynical and twisted, in the domestic mayhem in the city. Soon burn out sets in and one glove fits-all becomes the way, dealing with a radio response. These guys have seen it all, and their lives in the precinct were in constant jeopardy. As anyone can clearly see, I was being treated unfairly and all odds were against me; but I chose not to fight. I self-medicated with booze, drugs and gambling. I was emotionally immature and unbalanced. I became lonely and depressed, as if in a spell, having no way to feel better. I stopped the prescription pill popping. I did not realize the pains of dope sickness. The depression was intense and immobilizing for me. The business of transporting major executives all over the state began to crumble. It was the beginning of the end for me.

After shutting in for a month, I decided to throw in the towel, and do the unthinkable . . . . I needed to die as clinical depression had incapacitated me and turned me suicidal. I was stone cold sober, deciding to commit suicide June 4, 2004 in the Boston suburb of Waltham. I drove a brand New Lincoln Town car to a wooded area behind Totten Pond, just off route 128. I walked out and started to slice my wrists and arms with a box knife I purchased an hour earlier. Looking down, becoming upset and thinking I am wallowing in poison ivy. I can't explain; bleeding profusely and intent on death; and now I'm worrying about catching poison ivy! Roaming around for an hour and still alive, I got back in the Lincoln but still committed to end it all. I accelerated the car in the straightaway road behind the pond and pointed it into a telephone pole. The odometer reach 70mp when I impacted a telephone pole, slicing it in half, projecting me head first through the windshield, hitting the pole and landing 49 feet in front of the impact. I landed on my feet and remember being conscious, talking briefly to a person before lapsing into a three week coma, at a nearby hospital I.C.U unit. The fifteen hundred dollars or so in my pocket was missing. Had the airbags deployed or I was wearing a seat belt I would have been dead. The car had rolled over three times and burst into flames before exploding.

After three weeks in the nearby Woburn Leahy Clinic, I was transferred to Boston City Hospital for a three-month recovery plan. I had broken bones in my neck and back, fractured my skull, my hip, shoulder and broke many of my ribs; also suffering many internal injuries. My hip was my most troublesome injury of all, keeping me in traction for 60 days trying to mend.

My children were not permitted to see me, as my wife's lawyer said it would be too depressing for young children. How hateful these woman had become, was very striking. The children wrote me many sweet and thoughtful letters during my three months recovery. Grateful to be alive, I emerged from my tragic mistake without any noticeable handicaps or limitations, after my hospitalization was completed. Who gets projected 50 ft in the air through a windshield, bounced off a pole and survives without any permanent damage!? God was truly with me and did not want to take me at this time.

My wonderful employees did a fine job keeping the business running and pirating most of my accounts to their newly formed company. At least somebody that worked hard along side of me got the business. Without contracts anyone could have grabbed the major corporate accounts. With the pictures of the car after the accident, nobody thought I could come back to work running the business.

Out of the hospital, out of work two months and staying with mom, it was back to the condominium complex in the Dorchester neighborhood.

CHAPTER 6
A NEW BUSINESS

The canteen truck business caught my eye, and I proceeded to make a reasonable investment; to buy a truck and established route. Before the purchase, I had a chance to see for myself the eight stops and the revenue produced from them, all before the final purchase. I liked the idea of all cash, and being a mobile-restaurant for the working man. There would be a set schedule with this business and no weekends required. I sensed the seller was a bit of a snake. How could he stop "the invincible me" from turning out a big weekly profit? "The all mighty me" was not to be deterred by a fluffy con man. I figured I could always recreate the route with my own stops if his route fizzled out. This character defect turned into a soon to be enemy.

My truck was at the N.E. Commissary, in the working class city of Everett, just a mile north of Boston. The Commissary had all the charm of a back alley 19th century meatpacking house. There was however, good food in abundance, despite the draconian appearance and conditions of the 20 or so trucks that arrived there at 3:00 a.m., to load stock for each days work. A nasty Greek immigrant and his loyal family ran the entire store facility. The Greek even looked the part of a villain. Dark, black dyed hair, and a scar that ran eye socket to chin. He had a very bad foreign accent. Everyone remembered how he reminded us of Boris Badenoff, the bad guy from Bullwinkle and Rocky, the animated children's cartoon. His gambling addiction inspired many of his corporate business practices of robbing many vendors. Hood milk was owed over a million before they shut him off.

A straw owner had been planted because of the Greeks many arsons-for-profit convictions. Trucks parked at the Commissary were sometimes pilfered for food. The only surveillance cameras there were set-up to monitor the 30 or so Brazilian women who made the sandwiches at their stations. They would be reprimanded for too much talking and not enough working. The Greek had amassed a fortune in the 25-years of supplying the food trucks that fed Boston's workers. He was very arrogant and ruthless for a recent immigrant. I wondered, where was his muscle? Why are hardworking Americans submitting to this servant-master routine? I found out in the near future that his organized protection that was bought and paid for was in fact, the Everett Police Department. The local police were generously "greased" to watch his back. Also, another comfortable alliance was pact with the mayor of this open cesspool called Everett.

The man that sold me the route was a master of the old bait-and-switch con game. His intentions were to let me operate for a while and then drive me out of the commissary and business; keep it moving with another sucker, as he had done to the previous eight lads before me. His usual M.O. was not effective with me. When his construction sites folded, I would replace them with new ones I discovered through my extensive Boston knowledge learned in the Taxi years. Other honest men at the commissary had warned me of this mans scam, but I figured they would have to just about kill a cement head like me to get me to wavier. I was determined to operate a canteen truck route in Boston, despite watching a unified scheme to be rid of me.

The truck was well stocked and pleased my new and existing customers; with good food and good service for that first year. I always kept generous supplies of prescription painkillers on board, to ease the hurting construction workers. I was also consuming the pain pills, catching another sizeable habit by now. I was justifying my addiction; by the physical loading of the truck outside in the New England winters, and the fact that I had more broken bones than Evil Kneival. I had become my best customer. As they say, monkeys should not sell bananas. I was making good money and keeping each old and new stop happy.

The Greek and his partner in crime, Bobby S. were now ready to force me out and take over my new route. The first play was . . . to use the construction stewards and superintendents, his allies for many years, to start the troops complaining about the food. Soon the stewards at the largest stop were requesting a new truck to service them, jeopardizing the fifty thousand dollars I shelled out for the route. Bobby and I agreed to tell the customers that I worked for him and not risk new ownership to influence patronage.

There were a handful of Local 7 guys, steel workers, who had come to me, saying they were told to complain about the food and report of becoming sick. Bobby and crew had their program well rehearsed; he had succeeded with eight lads before me. The stewards would always help a man that fed them for free, over the decades, on "his trucks". I was not going to let Bobby's bait-and-switch game run away with the ball. I assembled a few thugs; I had to meet back at the furniture store and set out to have a chat with Bobby's Union Stewards. I had a large stop in Cambridge that a board of health inspector, called in by Bobby, tried to stop me from operating because of a lack of license. I quickly gave the food away for charity so I could feed my customers and fuck with the inspector and Bobby.

The men on my new crew were very muscular; looked, and were menacing. The three of us approached my largest stop, a large multimillion dollar addition to Mr. New Balance's buildings, and I told each steward "if my trucks were not here each day there would be no trucks at all". The stewards got the message, nodding up and down like toy dogs in the back of a car window. One of the Boston detail cops at the site gave me a cheer of solidarity, as he knew what was going on. The Greeks and Bobby had their money for the route. They wanted me gone and things got uglier.

The next day, one of the newer immigrants tried to stab me as I walked past a truck he was washing. He was lunging at me with a long carving knife from the truck. I managed to escape to my car and ride away. The incident rattled me on the ride back to Dorchester. It was February, and my pilot lights were being turned off at night as well, leaving the truck frozen, setting me back hours. I decided to call the Everett Police to make a report on the young Brazilian trying to carve me up like a Christmas Goose. I called on my way to work at 3 o'clock in the morning. The dispatcher had also heard about a "racial incident" that had happened up at the commissary, and told me he would not take out a complaint. Immediately now, Everett police were playing ball with the Greek and I needed to go elsewhere for help. The commissary was a huge cash cow, and everyone has a price, including the fine police of Everett.

It was also a well-known fact that Bobby had gone to high school with the Chief of Everett Police, John Nardone. Friendship or money; the bottom line . . . . they wanted me gone to take over the new and improved route.

Nearly a mile away from the commissary was another small working class city, Chelsea. I knew one officer from this city and he was now the chief, Frank Gusto. Frank used to drink with us out in Mission Hill, 25-years-ago. He was a regular at the "dating bar" Ed Burkes on Huntington Ave. I went to his office and began to explain what was happening at the city next door; and he listened very intently. He wanted nothing to do with the scenario and mentioned that it looked like a case for the F.B.I. He was not going against "Blue" personally, but he understood the problem and did the next best thing. Boston is such a small town.

Things got worse around the commissary. The other competition also wanted me gone. The new truck I had just purchased two months ago was falling apart. This was a cold winter, and driving down Commonwealth Ave and remarking how at least the cab was warm, then noticing six inch flames from the papers that caught fire from a cigarette match on the floor. The narcotics kept me alert and calm, stamping out the flames like there was nothing to it.

The F.B.I. seemed interested in the case for about a week. They assigned me to Bob; that was it . . . . fucking Bob. Never met him or got his last name. Bob asked me if there was evidence of O.C. on the premises. He wanted me to feel like a junior fed or something. I quickly replied "I see no evidence of organized crime on campus". Initially, they asked if I wanted protection from the violence, to come in and join the program. That was a missed opportunity in hindsight.

Bob called me in a week's time and gave me the bad news. "This office was no longer going to be involved with the canteen conspiracy" not giving any reason for the abrupt withdrawal of service. I was now 0 for 2 as Chelsea and the Feds didn't want involvement. I was feeling very small and without a country. What were my options now? I called Bob the Fed back and demanded answers. He said that having a lengthy criminal record and failing the test to be licensed to sell food were his reasoning. The Feds won't handle a case unless it is bullet proof.

I knew sitting next to Bobby S. during the test and asking for answers was not a good move. Bobby made sure the test was flunked. I'm sure the Feds were also informed of the massive amounts of narcotics consumed to keep functioning daily. The pills kept me wired to sound, and better able to defend my sinking ship. Active addiction did not help my decisions or rational thinking. I thought I was invincible. How did I expect to function with life's pitfalls, high on powerful narcotics? No question, these were evil men, hell-bent on robbing me, but, choosing not to be in the game by taking pills and drinking excessively was not the answer. I went back to the furniture store again to get some back up from the wanna-be gangsters and Lou Ronka was recommended for duty. He stuck to me like glue, providing back up and support at the commissary. I had another fistfight before he arrived.

Lou was a beefy Italian who knew how to act and what to do in every situation that came down the line. He always wore a North End Italian-logo sweatshirt, dark glasses and New York Yankees ball cap. He put on a Mafioso act at the commissary because the men who worked the trucks were used to dealing with the real thing. He intimidated most everyone, claiming alliance with real gangster factions based out in Roslindale. Lou became too expensive for me and I had to cut him out of the program on an everyday basis. Two days passed and I was ambushed on my way into the commissary.

On Feb. 3, 2006, I was driving the black Lincoln in the narrow strip between the trucks, on my way to my own, when Mike Cenci threw a cup of hot coffee into my open window, scalding me. The hot fluid splashed against my face and covered the leather seats. I threw my fourteen-dollar cigar out the window and headed for the Chelsea Police Department. I got to the Chelsea P.D. in 10 minutes and it was now 3:25 am. Both duty officers at the front desk were sound asleep when I started ringing the front buzzer for help. When the duty officers finally were awoken they called for EMT's to administer to my minor burns. The EMT's wanted to transport me to the hospital, but I didn't see the need; and the men had to be fed. The Chelsea police could not take a report because it was out of their jurisdiction. They said they would notify Everett for me. I doubled back to the N.E. Commissary holding a cold compress against the side of my face. An Everett cruiser met me and again refused to file a report without witnesses to corroborate my story. The Everett police were definitely in bed with the Greek. I managed to get through the day, feeding my two-hundred or so good customers, on this Friday in February. A concerned Bobby S. called to ask if I was O.K. How thoughtful of this human slime ball!

CHAPTER 7
15 MINUTES OF FAME

I returned to the commissary, parked the truck, and quickly peeled off a few sawbucks for the wash boy, waving bye-bye to the boys. An Everett police cruiser impeded my exit and a towering, well-built officer hopped out and began screaming at me to get out of the car. I rolled up the windows and hit the electric door locks, as another big officer came to the passenger window; both men were screaming and began kicking the windows in karate like fashion. Very calmly, I held up my index finger as if to oblige their requests, but that was not going to happen. They became more agitated and frenzied, and by now, each had drawn their silver 9mm gun and pointed them both at me. I was starring into the barrel of a loaded 9mm and trying to look into the officer's eyes. The cop looked more frightened then I. In a split second, I decided the chase was on. I shielded my hands over my face and put my Lincoln in reverse backing away very slowly and praying he would not squeeze off a round into my head. I was braced for the worst, but it never happened. I sped out the back gate, over the rugged terrain of the trucking route towards Chelsea. My "stinkin-thinking" of the moment was that Chelsea P.D. and the Feds would suddenly back my actions when the facts were investigated.

The on-scene police were given a hyped up report, totally false, of an employee who was fired earlier in the day and was now returning for violent revenge on the owners and employees. The real truth . . . . a sub-contractor was returning his truck and entering his car to go home after a week of hell at the N.E. Commissary. I was never an employee that could get fired. I had made the decision to flee

Everett, and take my chances with Chelsea P.D. or Boston, if I could get there in one piece. Five Everett cruisers lights and sirens blaring began to chase me down a truck route spotted with huge potholes everywhere. The chase was slow and I had thoughts of serious disbelief of what I had just got myself into. Of all the days not to have that fat fucking, dago, Lou on board as witness. I am sure Bobby S. had alerted his buddies in Everett police that today was a great day to take me down.

The slow 15-minute chase seemed like a police procession in a parade as more light-flashing squad cars and a news helicopter joined the chase. I was traveling 25 miles an hour in a big black Lincoln town car, stopping for lights and stop signs. At one point, a school crossing guard halted the whole chase as she waved the hexagon, red stop sign, and schoolchildren walked in front of my car. I let them pass waving my hands to each child, as they crossed in a business as usual fashion. I hit it as soon as they were safely on the other side and made into East Boston during rush hour, Friday afternoon stall. The sidewalks were lined with onlookers viewing the show unfolding before them. I decided to cut through a park and surrender to the Boston Police paddy wagons blocking a side street. I stepped about 100 yards in front of the wagons and got out with my hands up. As soon as my feet hit the pavement, my passenger window was smashed with a baton and I was wrestled to the ground, laying face down on the pavement and getting punched in the face until a Boston cop told the Everett police to stop. They bundled me up in cuffs and threw a sweatshirt over my head as they led me to the squad car.

The ride back to Everett was an interesting one, as my newfound friends began to pump me for information. I felt a great sense of relief surrendering, after what seemed to be longer than a 15 minute reported chase through Everett and Chelsea, and landing in East Boston. I remained calm and at ease while the Everett cops tried to be ever so nice to me, in hopes of gaining information that they had already received from their rat friends, whom they had grown up with, whom worked along side me. I just wanted a smoke and to lay down for a while, emotionally exhausted. Bobby S. had briefed his cop friends on who I was and they felt bad about taking the working the man down. Money can ease many guilty feelings and the Everett police were definitely greased to help with the pain.

Back at the station, the higher-ranking cops left the door to the small cell open and gave me smoke and a newspaper. They tried to be hospitable and we shared a few laughs as S. must have told them how I was always joking around. Bail was set at 700 cash, which was not bad after receiving an assorted menu of serious charges for my car chase. Lou was up to bail me out in about 2 hours time. We took the subway back to my Dorchester condominium. On the ride back, I expressed my regrets about not having him on board on this tragic Friday. We stopped at the Liquor store on the way up Savin Hill for supplies.

The two local Boston papers and 3 news stations covered my 15 minute romp on Boston's north side (East Boston), on an otherwise tranquil, and obviously, uneventful news day in the Hub. My ex-wife, very rarely bothered with the local news. Someone, thank God, mailed her the article from the Boston Globe detailing the horrific car chase and assault on the two innocent Everett police officers. She, without hesitation applied and received a new restraining order, adding the children for their safety. The Greek held my truck, my wife held the kids.

The new business venture had caused some major wreckage. I sent Lou across the street on Feb 14 with clothing and Valentines candy for the children, purchased before the new restraining order was implemented. He also presented some paperwork to alert Juanita of my appeal of the new order. Lou was met at the door, said nothing, and returned to party central. This seemingly harmless act was a huge mistake in the state of Missesgetstochoositt. It was a direct third party violation of a civil order now becoming a criminal offense, punishable by two years in jail. Alana Kline, my wife's "man-eating" lawyer, was first to deliver the good news of the new violation, over the phone. The top-dog for the very powerful Boston School Teachers Union had delivered a 1st round knockout punch in the prolonged divorce trial.

CHAPTER 8
Time Out

I was arrested on a Thursday in Dorchester for a third-party restraining violation. My bail in Everett was revoked until a trial date. The local police handle an enormous responses to battered woman and they treated me as a usual scumbag suspect. They were also very much aware of the canteen truck debacle and painted me in as a dangerous criminal.

It was President's weekend and I would remain in the barren police station for four long days, shivering in the cold cell without blanket or pillow to sleep. The four days spent at C-II station lock-up seemed worse than the ensuing 12 months spent in county jail. Lou was now left in charge to retrieve the truck and by imminent domain, remain at the condominium in Dorchester. His drug addiction became out of control. He sold everything that was not bolted down. During my journey in county jail, the bank sold my condominium, which was emptier than a handball court. In two years time, Lou would overdose on pills and leave behind two grieving, young adult children.

I was moved to Nashua Street Jail on the Charles River, near the Boston Garden. The bail revocation was just a formality as one could not walk until the case was disposed of in Dorchester District Court. My hands and legs were shackled and standing before the judge, I would remain "bound in the cheap jewelry," even at trial." Can one get a fair shake, bound, wearing a one-piece orange jump suit?" I was very grateful to be out of precinct C-11; transferred into the much more humane environment of Nashua St. Jail. Nashua Street Jail, ironically, was my first stop on my canteen route and many correctional officers still had open tabs. In less than two months time, I was now an inmate awaiting trial, without bail. The officers were very puzzled and they sided with me, especially if they owed money from my route.

The jail was relatively new. It seemed relaxed with little tension on the surface. The population awaiting trial was mixed, by age and race. Men stayed with their own kind. I spent most of the time outside the cell with other white guys from Southie, Dorchester, Hyde Park and smaller cities to the north. We played cards, chess, and tried to keep optimistic about our upcoming trials, on the short period of time spent out of the shared cell. Gambling on sports and card games was big. Each unit had a bookie to place bets on sporting events. The currency was usually canteen food purchased at the jail weekly. Outside money could be placed in the canteen accounts to cover bets as well. There were few fights and most of the people that were dragged off the unit, were for possession of drugs or homebrew. Cigarettes were illegal and one smoke cost five dollars. I was amazed and at the same time embarrassed at how many friends and neighbors were employed at Nashua Street.

I felt defeated. Juanita, my significant other for fourteen years, had betrayed me and made me an insignificant number in the system. I was isolated from society for the first time at 43-years-old. Detoxing from the massive tissue-dependency of the pain pills was rough. After six irritable, sleepless, nights the narcotics left my system and I began to eat and regain strength, on this forced vacation. After 97 days, I was lugged into Dorchester District Court to answer the charge of a third party restraining order violation. Dorchester was a busy court, always packed with defendants from the most blighted inner-city landscapes. Eighty-five percent of the defendants were Black or Hispanic.

The conviction rate was extremely high, as only wealthy drug dealers could afford legal representation. Most cases were plea bargains, and the question after admission of guilt would be how much jail time to be served.

This court was the birthplace of Domestic Violence Prevention; beating of woman was very common in this district. A minority professor commented, in a class that I would take years down the road, that physical beating were an accepted practice, in the past, especially for some black relationships.

Sometime before noon on Dec 9th, I was led from the bullpen in Dorchester District Court. My hands and legs shackled, wearing an orange jumpsuit, to hear my fate on the restraining order violation. The judge was Hispanic and he appeared irritable, in a foul mood. Juanita was called to testify and was immediately handed a box of tissues by the accommodating bailiff. The water works had commenced; it was show time as she wept and sobbed from start to finish. It is a theatrical gift to cry on queue, and her well-coached display drew an outpour of emotion from the court. I sensed the gig was up, but kept optimistic feelings in the tense moments that lay ahead. Certainly, the 95 days in the city jail would be penalty enough for an alleged act of gifting my two young girls. Could that much trauma be triggered by having Lou waddle over with Valentine Day presents for my children? Kline had directed her client well. It was difficult to contain myself in the courtside bullpen, as lie after lie followed crockadile teardrops and sobs.

I stood tall and stared stoically straight ahead, ignoring the judge's commands to be seated. My court-appointed public-pretender lawyer sprung into action to cross-examine the witness. "Was your husband a good provider"? Oh, yes he was" Juanita replied without hesitation. "What was he wearing when he dropped the gifts?" Just as quickly, "a red baseball hat and a blue jacket", Kline had prepped her well. I despised the color red and never wore ball caps. The judge and the courtroom bought the charade, for the most part. Many of the females were sobbing along with Juanita. A small gathering of black men in the back of the courtroom were in a knee-slapping laughter/banter as they pointed in my direction. Had they been through a similar debauchery here in this court? I felt some male solidarity, but I was not thinking clearly at this point in time. My fate was sealed. Judge Ronquilla barked out "15 months house of corrections", slamming the gavel as if he were trying to break it to fucking pieces. Even Johnny Cochran would not have helped me on that day. The Boston Teachers Union had led another unfortunate "lamb to the slaughter".

With the court case from the Everett police chase pending, I was off to the notorious South Bay Jail for a little over a year, receiving time credits for awaiting trial at Nashua St Jail. The court officers were sympathetic as they led me to the packed wagon. They knew I was a family man, caught up in a nasty divorce, not the usual gangbanger that they dealt with each day. As soon as we were outside, a condoling officer lit a smoke for me and commented how "all broads are liars on the stand." I was still in shock! My mind drew a blank.

On March 29, 2007, I landed at South Bay House of Corrections, in the middle of Boston's South End. It was adjacent to one of the cities busiest highways, Route 93. I remember gazing out the window at motorists caught in stand-still gridlock, wanting to give my left arm to be stuck out there with them. Three men crammed into a cells, poorly designed for two. "How could the state allow such primitive housing?" I thought I was in fucking Bangladesh or some third world country. Remember, a hop across the river were the world renowned educational facilities of Harvard and M. I. T.

With one of the highest incarceration rates in the country, somehow this state was making money. Criminal justice is big business; my advice would be avoiding arrest.

The 1st housing block was new mans block, where you were orientated and locked down for 23-hours a day, for a thirty day "initiation to the Bay". The flavor of the month was banana yellow, the color of our jumpsuits. My cell was on the fourth floor, with a view of our steeple at St Margaret's Church, four miles away in Dorchester. I tried to remember better times when I looked at the steeple for hope. The food was not suitable for human consumption and served in starvation portions, another component of the punishment mentality of the jail. To survive one had to rely on the jails cash-cow-run canteen industry.

I thought I recognized one of the two young black men who were now living beneath me, in 3 stacked bunks. I asked Reggie "where are you from? Where do I know you from?" His response was, "Look man, do you and leave me alone". Our other guest was a frequent flyer, and knew how to pass time. He never shut up; I think Martin could talk under water. Reggie opened up after five days, dropping the hard guy veneer. He had fifteen years in the state prison system on his resume. I wondered how such a slight built lad could have survived the deadly jungles of the Massachusetts state prisons. If you know the right people, ally with them, then you will not be victimized and sent to protective custody. This is where the frail and undesirables are banished. This sink or swim reality was not as severe on the county level; however, this was not charm school either.

When the cop came to the door, after my first week of stay, he asked to have "Reggie Bly come forward" to the door. That was the missing piece to the puzzle; Reggie was one of my kids at Connelly Detention Ctr. in Roslindale, from the early 80's. He was also the cousin of Jeffery Bly, who stalked and murdered a high profile prosecutor in Boston. His cousin was convicted, and is doing a life sentence. Reggie did not want to be linked or confused with him, so he tried to remain under the radar. We talked of the good ole' days at D. Y.S.

My first major problem at the jail surfaced in just two weeks time. Reggie had clipped an extra cup of juice off the table, on the way back to the cell. An angry sergeant slapped the cup out of his hand and pressed his mouth against his ear, for the walk all the way back to our cell. The older, balding cop also berated Reggie with racial slurs and taunts. I made another classic, impulsive bad decision . . . I tried to help my boy Reggie from this total degradation. The incident did not daunt Reggie one bit. I told the sergeant "back off or contend with me" The cop stopped at the door and yelled over "lock these mother fuckers down!" All inmates moved quickly into their cells, like scared mice to their holes. I felt an initial victory as I thwarted the attack on Reggie. I then set out to relax on my bunk and wallow in my heroic achievement. Within 5 minutes there were seven goons outside my door, barking my name out, to "come forward before they cracked the door". In a high-pitched, mock female voice replying, "He's in a meeting, come back in an hour". I heard a few chuckles from the crew outside the door and leaped to the front as the door flew open. Two large goons grabbed an arm apiece and spun me around as they clicked on the handcuffs. A third cop started banging my head against the wall with loud thuds. They then forced my upper body over the railing as if to throw me over to a certain death. The circus in front of my cell caused some commotion on the tier, as various profanities were hurled at the cops. Some of the other inmates began singing "throw him off!" in a rhythmic chant. They marched me off, cuffed hands behind my back, to "the hole" to await my sanctions. The move team that escorted me to the discipline unit knew some of my friends that worked in the system; neighborhood guys, they tried to humanize the situation. They gave me some advice, "nobody ever sticks out ones neck for fellow inmates!!." These cops knew it was my rookie season, or first time in "the big house". They said they could make things easier when I got out of the hole. One cop had brought me some ice, for the golf ball sized lump on my forehead.

The hole was not that bad at all; I had my own room and was locked-down the same 23-hours a day as the yellow unit. The substandard meals were delivered to my door. We were allowed out but we were cuffed and shackled, before we went to the shower and made phone calls. Writing letters was a lot cheaper and did not evoke the stress of a phone conversation. The phone was another money-suck that the jail made money on. A local call could cost over 5 dollars a wack. Many men lived on the "Ma Bell" stress box, trying to fix situations on the outside they had no control over. Contraband, in the form of a book was left under my mattress for me to enjoy. The book was spotted by a crack agent of the correctional staff. My only grain of stimulus was disposed of, into the barrel on-wheels in front of my cell. I would never know if that lady and her camels would make it across the dangerous Australian outback.

After a week, my time in the hole began to wear on me. Out for one hour each day, shackled, sent home the message. This was "their" house, and they had rules no matter how unfair or archaic. The integrity of the institution was not going to be compromised by me. Being in jail in genera1, to me, was like being buried alive. I was not able to "relax and enjoy the vacation" like the other inmates, who become institutionalized over the years; who embraced the predictability of a controlled environment. This was just a stop on their life journey; they did the time easily, without stress. I heard one experienced inmate say "The Bay was like a playground with bad food". In the hole, I sang aloud songs from the 70's and 80's, to keep from losing my sanity, and sinking into depression.

I would remain in the jail within a jail for eight more days, for the disturbance on new mans unit, the week before. A few cell doors down were pure fireworks. An inmate wanted a transfer out of South Bay to someplace better, which, was just about anywhere. He was pissing out the door, throwing milk cartons loaded with feces or aptly named "shit bombs". He would kick his door for hours, as he ranted like a mad man. He knew if he persisted, they would transfer him to another stop in the county system. Other counties had more money than ours, as Suffolk was the poorest in the state. The wealthier communities were much better places to do time. Food and housing were much more desirable in Middlesex County, which was the wealthiest county. Inmates coined its jail the "Billerica House of Pancakes." There was also a good work release program during transition to freedom.

I recognized his voice, the Italian-rhythm of the East Boston dialect. Yes, another one of my success stories from D.Y.S., doing life on the installment plan. I had worked with over 500 troubled youths, now 30-years later I am reunited with two of them, in my own mid-life stumble. In my remaining months, I would encounter three more lads from the youth facility. Only Bruno, in the hole now with me, showed any emotion and gratitude for my futile efforts to make life better for adolescent boys caught up in criminal mischief, in the early eighties. Bruno was the recipient of many goodies and privileges because he was Italian. He did not whine about his predicament. We talked briefly through the doors and he began to calm down. He admitted to being very institutionalized as he recalled the good treatment he received by me.

Food, smokes, and reading material are big when you are locked up. Inside of about a half hour, the move team came with a German Sheppard to take Bruno to his next stop in the county system. It was business as usual. Everyone present had been there before; things went as if it was rehearsed. Bruno was removed without force. He was strapped to wheel chair tighter than a clam with lockjaw. He yelled back to me that I could find him "up the Heights in Eastie". I yelled back "God bless you! Stay strong!" This lad, who was about 40-years-of-age, is a percentage that will stay "trapped in the system" for the majority of his life, warehoused by the state, eager to keep him. For the most, Bruno is a great commodity in the system, and has the ability to navigate for survival. Over the years, inmates even bond with staff, some whom are humane, just wanting to get through the day without mayhem. Count fifty bodies at the beginning of the shift, on the tier, and the same fifty when they leave; this is more the mentality at the state prison where Bruno spent close to twenty years.

The more institutionalized the more valuable the inmate becomes. These programmed "pets" stay in the boundaries of the routine. In other words, the situation is accepted, and they breeze through and enjoy the vacation. Jail is not a punishment but a "relaxing way of life." "Do the time and do not let the time do you," is a common slogan in "the can." Most criminal behaviors are the direct result of active addiction and substance abuse disorders. The state and federal governments continue to pour monies into punishment, ignoring prevention and reentry programs. People are being sent to jail for crimes that would not be arrest able offenses back in "the day". Outside of organized crime, only a handful are professional criminals, the jails are full of desperate addicts; and their pathetic ways of obtaining money to get high or behaving badly while intoxicated. Nowadays, inmates in the state's maximum state prisons resemble suburban high school lacrosse team members.

Unofficial records of what it cost the state budget is over forty-thousand dollars a year to warehouse an inmate, not counting for medical costs and some other programs offered. Rehabilitation at South Bay was crude as programs were few and not taken seriously by staff. In the near future, I would discover good old-fashioned A.A. (Alcoholics Anonymous); would be the best correction for my listing ship. My feeling, "the best social program is a job", though, there are not enough jobs at livable wages for the citizens of this country. I refuse to label any human as "an illegal".

CHAPTER 9
THE PROGRAM

My trial in Everett was scheduled for next month, up in Malden District Court. After two months at South Bay, I was settling into the routine of jail life, feeling confident that the county jail time could be done, that I would eventually be free after the numbers from Malden came in. I had been advised from some of the more experienced inmates, to try to have the sentence run concurrent and plead out. The deal was worked out and my time ran concurrent by a sympathetic judge. I would now be eligible for early release or parole at the halfway point in my sentence or about four more months. On an otherwise normal day at the Bay, I was escorted to a conference room across, on the other side of the jail. A representative for the Feds and State police greeted me with a warm "how d'ya do?". The outside stimulus and attention was welcome, and I was really intrigued by their presence. Of most cops, their mission was to" help me out". How very thoughtful of these "messengers of good intentions." "We are working on indictments on the Everett police who forced you out", was their calling card. All that these men wanted from me was to roll over like a circus elephant, telling them of all the drug dealers I knew of and about.

First off, I only knew small-time street dealers had pled out and accepted the deal. I apologized and remained silent. I told them "maybe down the line I could help". They had chosen the wrong guy for this police work and left with the usual fake pleasantries, nothing for nothing with these guys. A few years down the line an under-cover state police detective pulled me over on Broadway in Southie. This guy hopped in the passenger side and told me of the criminal complaints brought against Everett police and he actually thought my arrest was a huge injustice. He shook my hand and told me to drive him down a narrow side street so I would not look like an informant.

I survived the County jail and was paroled to a remote island 5 miles off shore, only accessible by a bridge that was badly decaying. The parole officer, who drove a young lad and me, got started in the Boston School System. He knew Juanita my ex, as he worked briefly at the Blackstone School in the South End, as a custodian. There was my in, my leg-up so-to-speak! Mike Joyce would look after me and guide me through the next six months remaining on the parole. Arriving in the middle of Boston Harbor, on a magnificent, bright spring day was a sensory overload. Leaving the dark, dreary cages set in concrete; for me this was an ultimate high. It was like my first trip to the Caribbean taken in happier times, when the girls were younger. The white sands, bright blue tranquil ocean, and the warm evening breeze stoking my Cuban cigar, while I sipped a rum libation could only compare. This was truly a welcomed paradise! What a spectacular view of the Boston skyline and inner harbor.

Unfortunately, the water temperatures were about 45 degrees. The coarse gravel beaches were off limits to island residents for liability reasons. The Island, named for its shape, hence, it was dubbed Long Island, often confused with the famous New York borough. It was at the mouth of the inner harbor on one side of a very narrow, busy shipping channel. The massive tankers with tugs on each side seemed close enough to touch. The jets to and from Logan Airport flew low to the island as we were only a mile away from the landing strips in the extreme inner harbor.

Long Island had some history as a civil war burial ground. In the late thirties until the fifties, it housed quarantined tuberculosis patients. The old, four story buildings were perfect for housing homeless and recovering addicts. One of the few programs slated for men coming back to society named Reentry, was my first stop on the island. The program was designed for men to learn and participate in recovery. The living quarters were like a college dorm, although located in the basement of a homeless shelter. There were twenty men along side me, learning about recovery, trying to fit back into society, and avoid the legal system. All the men were on parole. Any rule infraction would send you back to the "Big House" for further "reflection". This unit was a therapeutic community that had many, very punitive rules, which sent 50% of the men back to jail. Every morning in group Mike Joyce lugged another little Indian back to jail. In the therapeutic treatment facility, every little thing is a rule violation. Discipline and a steady diet of the A.A. program were big items on the menu. We attended four meetings a day; three off campus meetings in the city, after the morning "share" group that was for residents. It was the daily schedule. The program was created by three addicts, in recovery; all who had over 30 years combined time in state and federal prisons. Vans ran every two hours. If one missed the van, used drugs, acted unruly, or get into a fight, back you went.

This was the "vacation" to me, as I had some time to "relax" before looking for work. It was a mild, dry spring and we were allowed outside to a grass covered hill and basketball court about the size of two football fields. The bright sun and proximity to the ocean was perfect for lying atop a picnic table to catch sun, like a beach bum. I had a feeling of accomplishment, as if I had been away fighting in a foreign war. Now was time to decompress and enjoy the Island's lush greenery and the beautiful Atlantic that surrounded us. This was my long anticipated reward for survival in the "Massachusetts day care dungeons for drug addicts."

The barrage of A. A. meetings had penetrated the denial front. I heard my story a dozens of times. The real tough guys met life on life's terms; without booze or drugs to numb the insults of life. I had accepted that life would be better if I put the plug in the jug and surrendered to win. I was not fighting the good fight when I was self-prescribing a mixed bag of feel-good drugs. I would soon learn the meaning of serenity, one day at a time as a better way to cope. We were told to "give up one thing and you can have everything." The rum was out of the fruitcake. I was determined to take the program seriously. The substances were my crutch to navigate the difficult times and now I needed spirituality to replace the drugs. The progress was little and slow.

The job search was abysmal, between the sagging economy and my criminal record. I would attend all the workshops for the offenders in downtown Boston each day. The program people suggested a get-well job for my aid in the recovery process. I gave up and took the advice. I started working in the island laundry room, stuffing dryers as fast as I could, for eight hours a day. In two months time I had enough of the job, realizing there was "no future in dryer stuffing at minimum wage."

I returned to a place that I had spent most of my summers growing up, Brookline Mass., home of "The Country Club". At age 45, I was not the oldest caddy at the club. By early spring, I was a welcomed employee. They needed loopers until school broke, and I backed into a weeks pay of hard work at historical Brookline, home of the epic caddy who conquered the great Harry Vardon, as an amateur to win the U. S. Open. Francis Quimet grew up right across the street from the club. He pulled off the most incredible sporting upset of the century, back in 1913 at Brookline. It took two hours to get to the club by seven each morning. I was as welcome as genital herpes by the veteran caddies, who had spent decades in the trenches with the Harvard Hackers. A new horse in the barn could jeopardize potential work for these men, I could feel the squeeze. A four-hour stroll in the summer heat with an extra fifty pounds of the latest golfing gear was the bill-of-fare. It was a physical test of my endurance and stamina. My assignment was to lead two financial moguls around the most prestigious course in the world so they could thoroughly enjoy the game of golf. This was the playground of the Cabot's, Lodges, Lowell's, Olmsteads, and Saltenstalls of the industrial revolution. I was their personal valet for four grueling hours. I would give them all the yardage distances and read the puts on every green. On one occasion, I even caddied for the head of the F.B.I. and his henchmen in tow. I never discussed my run in with the G-men, but made jokes to his protection crew of how Whitey made fools of the Bureau's Boston branch. Two golf carts of heavily armed agents followed Director Mueller the entire round. There were very few skilled golfers under the straps being carried. I could beat most, and most could not hit the ball into the ocean. This was a good job out in the sun and fresh air around the game I had loved for so long. I was back in the Short Grass Again. The End

www.ingramcontent.com/pod-product-compliance
Lightning Source LLC
Chambersburg PA
CBHW030520290526
45786CB00004B/1552